CU00409720

Purple Ronnie's

Little Book to say

I LOVE
YOU
LOTS

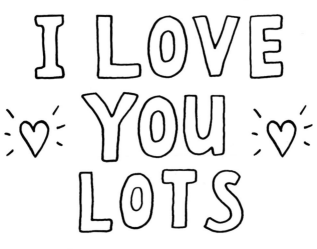

by Purple Ronnie

First published 2010 by Boxtree
an imprint of Pan Macmillan Ltd
Pan Macmillan, 20 New Wharf Road, London N1 9RR
Basingstoke and Oxford
Associated companies throughout the world
www.panmacmillan.com

ISBN 978-0-7522-2717-7

Some of the material in this book was previously published as *Purple Ronnie's Little Poems to Say I Love You*,
Purple Ronnie's Little Guide for Lovers and *Purple Ronnie's Little Book of Love Poems*

A CIP catalogue record for this book is available from the British Library.

Printed and bound by Proost, Belgium

'Purple Ronnie'™ created by Giles Andreae. The right of Giles Andreae and Janet Cronin
to be identified respectively as the author and illustrator of this work has been asserted by them
in accordance with the Copyright, Designs and Patents Act 1988.

Visit **www.panmacmillan.com** to read more about all our books
and to buy them. You will also find features, author interviews and
news of any author events, and you can sign up for e-newsletters
so that you're always first to hear about our new releases.

a poem to say

I Love You Lots

I want to say I love you-lots!

But I can't, I don't know
why

The words just get all
tangled up

Is it that I'm shy?

a poem about
The One

The first time that I ever
met you

My body just sort of went
"wow!

I know that's the person
I know that's the one!"

And you know - it's still
saying it now

a love poem about

Shoes

You could be at the
football
Or even on the booze
Instead you're at the
shopping mall,
Checking out the shoes

a poem to say

You're Sexy

There's something I wanted
to tell you
I hope you don't mind
if I do
There's no-one who's half
as deliciously gorgeous
Or scrumptiously sexy as
you

a poem about

My Bubbling Brain

The reasons that I love you?
Let's see- where shall I start?
There's reasons bubbling
            from my brain
And hammering in my heart

Girls Beware:-

Most men need a lesson in how to make you feel special

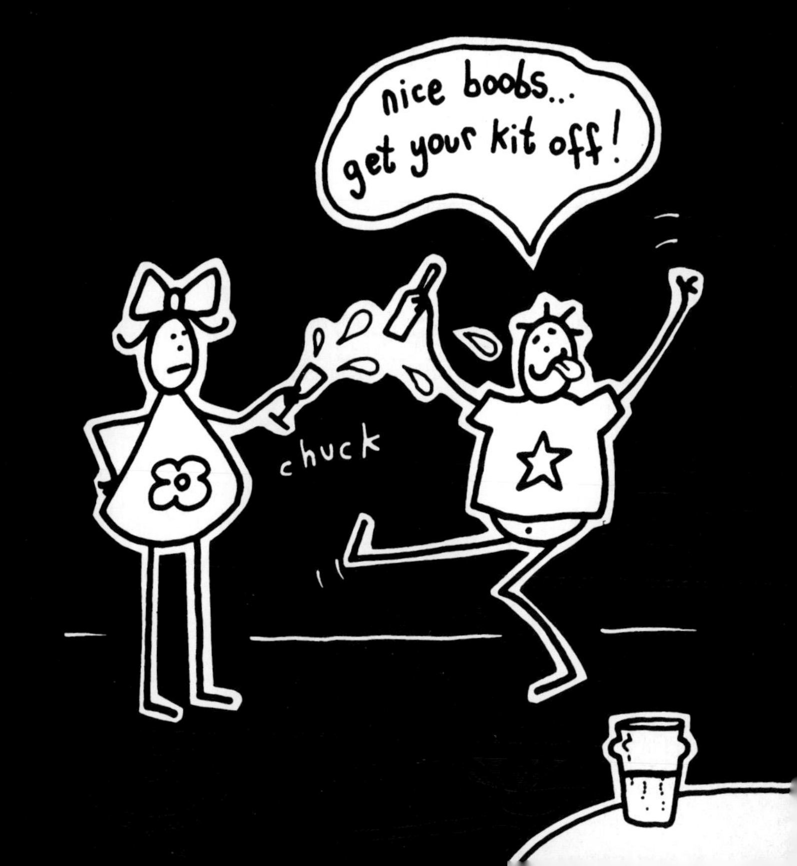
nice boobs...
get your kit off!
chuck

my love for yoooooooou
is aaalll the tiiimme
my looooove
...urm... I'm going to be late for work
in a rush
loved up
tap tap

a poem about

My Love For You

Valentine's Day is full
of flowers
and sloppy cards that
rhyme
But I just want to sing
to yooooooou...
My love is all the time

Try to look after
her when she's ill.
It shows that you
really care

you not feeling very well
I made you a little snack, my love
my special soup

a poem about
↓
Being in Love

Whenever I'm with you
My heart starts to thump
And I come over wonky
        and flustered

I try to stay calm
But pour milk on my toast
And butter my coffee
        with mustard

Sometimes it's good to pay your lover an unexpected compliment

<u>Being Fancied</u>

If you want people to fancy you - it is best to be as mysterious as possible

a poem about

Why I Love You

You may think that I love
you
Because you glow and glisten
But what to me brings
joy and glee
Is when I talk, you listen!

nod
nod
...blah...blah...
fangletweeked the
crankshaft...
blah... leaky
gimble...

Men Beware :-

Girls always have sneaky ways of catching the men they fancy

you're so cool and handsome and funny and clever and tough and manly etc etc etc
Smitten

Show your devotion
by letting your girl
go on about her
friends to you...

... blah... blah...
and Sheena said to me...
...blah... blah...
oh really?
fluster
flap
← v. bored

Special Tip for Men

Girls like their lovers to be romantic and exciting...

...It is not <u>always</u> best to be incredibly skilful

a poem about

My Life With You

Before I ever met you
Fun times were rare
                 and few
But now my life is bliss
                 and joy

And all because of you

a poem about

Great Pants

Underwear is fun to wear
Especially saucy scanties
So, just to say
Hey, come and play
Oooh look - some lacy panties!

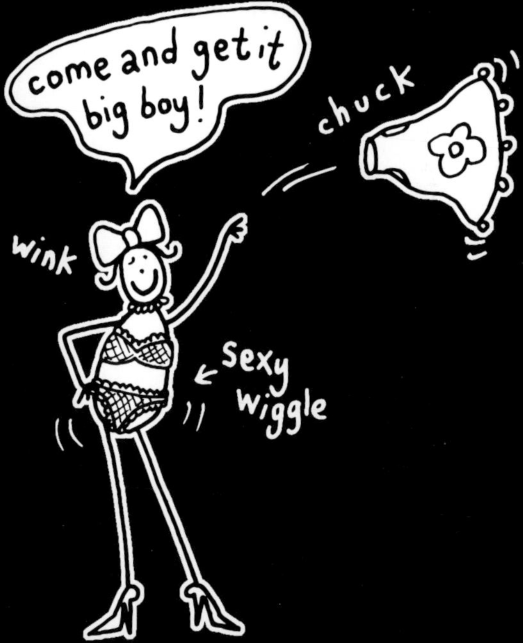
come and get it big boy!
chuck
wink
sexy wiggle

a poem to say

I Love You

This poem says I Love You
With you my life is sweet
Except when you start
farting
Or forget to wash your
feet!

Girls really love it if you're nice to them in front of their friends

a soppy poem to say

You're Lovely

Every time I see your face
It's like a lovely gift
At every view my heart
goes "Oooh!"
And gives a little lift!

me feeling gooey about you
you being gorgeous
gaze
Oooh!
flutter

a poem about

My Heart

My heart was like a
    treasure chest
You had the magic key

You came along and clicked
    the lock

And now the treasure's free

a poem to say

Be My Valentine

I could drink a case of you

If you were fizzy wine

To use plain talk you

pop my cork!

So be my Valentine!

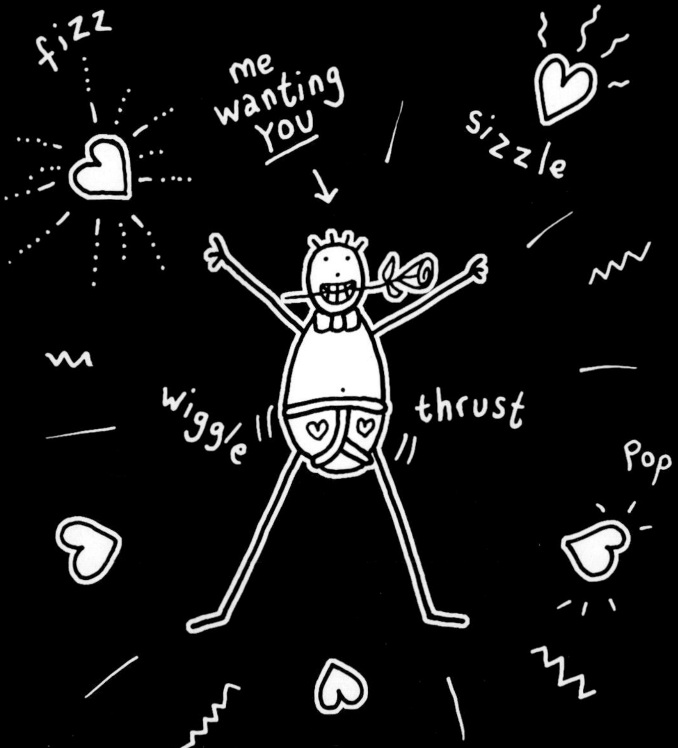
fizz
me wanting YOU
sizzle
wiggle
thrust
Pop

a poem about not loving
Curry Farts

When you're in Love, you
love ALL of a person
You don't sort the right from
the wrong
But I can't love the smell
of my man's curry farts
'Cos they make such a horrible
pong!

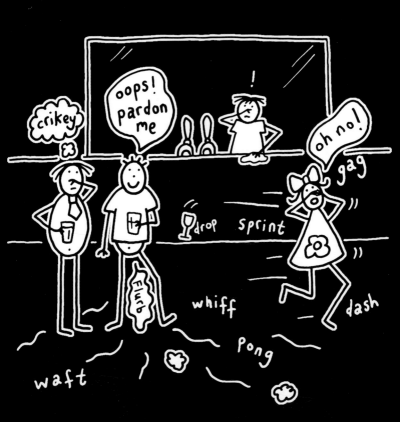

a poem about
Falling in Love

It's funny how people say
"falling in love"
Cos I never felt any pain
And falling in love
Felt so lovely with you
That I think we should
do it again

a poem about feeling

Smiley Inside

Love makes you feel all
cuddly and warm
Love makes your tongue get
all tied
It makes you go wobbly
And weak at the knees
And all sort of smiley
inside

a poem to say

You Make me Dizzy

I just want to tell you
I love you so much
That each time you walk
through the door
My heart gets so fizzy, my
head goes all dizzy
And Love knocks me flat on
the floor!

a poem about

Ravishing You

I'd like to go up to
the bedroom

And quietly turn down
the light

Then put on some beautiful
music

And ravish you madly
all night

Give your lover a
surprise gift – women
LOVE surprises

a romantic poem for

You

♡ ♡

When you're away I have to
say
My life's just not complete
When you're around I feel
the ground
Give way beneath my feet

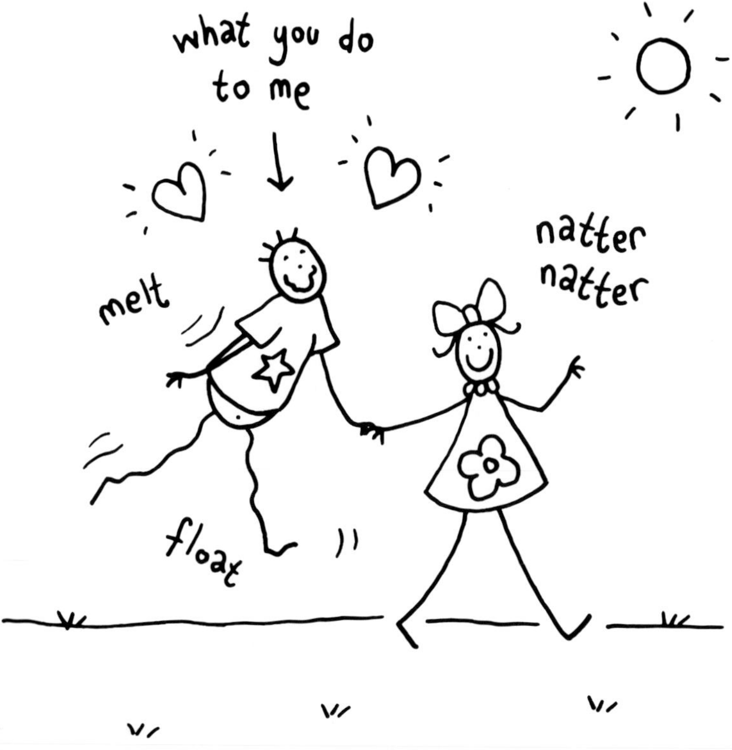
what you do
to me
melt
float
natter
natter

a poem to say

I Really Love You

I don't mind standing at the sink

To scrub at pans and pots

I'll pamper you because it's true

I really love you- lots!

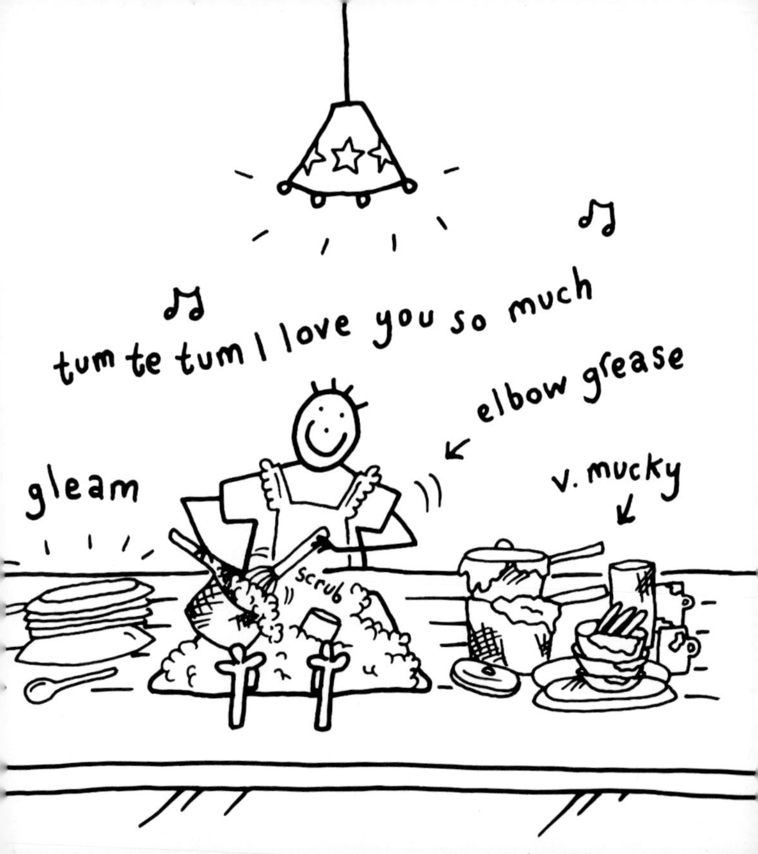
tum te tum I love you so much
elbow grease
gleam
v. mucky
scrub